ONCE AGAIN FOR
THUCYDIDES

ONCE AGAIN FOR THUCYDIDES

BY PETER HANDKE

TRANSLATED FROM THE GERMAN
BY TESS LEWIS

A NEW DIRECTIONS BOOK

Book design by Sylvia Frezzolini Severance
Manufactured in the United States of America
New Directions Books are printed on acid-free paper.
Noch einmal für Thukydides originally published in German in 1995 by Residenz Verlag. First published as New Directions Paperbook 25(NDP25) in 2008
Published simultaneously in Canada by Penguin Books Canada Limited

Library of Congress Cataloging-in-Publication Data

Handke, Peter.
   [Noch einmal für Thukydides. English]
   Once again for Thucydides / Peter Handke; translated by Tess Lewis.
      p. cm.
   ISBN 0-8112-1388-9 (alk. paper)   ISBN: 978-0-8112-1776-7
   I. Lewis, Tess.   II. Title.
   PT2668.A5N613   1998
   838'.91403—dc21   98-17509
                     CIP

New Directions Books are published for James Laughlin
by New Directions Publishing Corporation
80 Eighth Avenue, New York 10011

CONTENTS

FOR THUCYDIDES

On March 23, 1987, a leaf in the evergreen ivy climbing the side of a house on the Felsenberg seemed wilted. When a man's shadow fell on the leaf, it rose up, spreading wings infinitely yellower underneath—the strongest color seen in a long time. Then, a second brimstone butterfly flew around the corner of the house, a twitching shadow on the wall. The butterflies alit, revealing a pair of dark spots on their veined, lemon-yellow wings, one dot above the other; their heads retained ·

something of their former caterpillar states. Throughout the winter they had hung unnoticed in the bushes, rolled up like cigarettes. Next to one of the butterflies, a first bee landed suddenly. Again, as the butterfly flew off, its underwings emitted their deep shine into the world, forcing one's glance back into a look around. This was after the ten o'clock news on the radio. The sun grew warmer, and both butterflies disappeared. By midday, deep in the front garden, the granular snow of the firn began to stir. The grains of snow began to topple as if of their own will. They fell away, rolling to the side, and grew more diaphanous and transparent with each glance. Across the entire blanket of snow and throughout the garden there was a constant, endless jolting, lurching, beginning-to-flow, trickling, and—if one brought one's ear close—a rustling. It was the snow melting. Some of the grains settled on the incline, gleaming under the warm sun like the concave mirrors of tiny cosmic telescopes. At the same time, the blanket of snow sagged visibly, and between the several blades of new grass piercing it. The rocket of a first crocus flashes up, still half-shrouded in leaves, the deep blue tip aimed towards the equally blue outer space. Seen through a magnifying glass, the crystallized firn was full of soot. These were the events of the morning of March 23, 1987.

THE PIGEONS OF PAZIN

I spent the night of the 22nd to the 23rd of August, 1987, in the central Istrian town of Pazin, in a hotel on the edge of a rocky precipice, a so-called "sink-hole," at the foot of which, far below, Dante is said to have entered into the Inferno. Someone was still playing the accordion after midnight, and a small owl, so timid it seemed tame, hooted continuously in the dark pines along the sink-hole's rim. Then in the darkest night, a rooster crowed, reminding me of the enormous bumble-bee I had seen the day before, stirring up pale bluebells. I remembered the cicada in an apple tree and St. Martin on a fresco in Beram's solitary church. I had always been offended by this saint who cut his robe in half, but now, for the first time, I began to understand him. Towering above the poor, naked beggar who smiles like a half-wit, St. Martin divided his cloak and, reaching down from his horse, draped it around the man's shoulders. The enormous saint looks down sorrowfully upon such "conditions."

The next day in Pazin was a Sunday. Tides of silence washed over the city so that the gurgling of pigeons reigned high up in the trees, especially in the cedars. At the bottom of another sink-hole (the area is known for these vertical pits), I came upon dead trees standing in a lake covered with pea-green algae. Later, at the train station, more than a few of the young Yugoslavian faces appeared disfigured, if only because of the gaps between their teeth, and I thought of the petrifying, Medusa-like gaze which I myself, already exposed, sometimes used unconsciously or even against my will, in order to expose others. I knew I had to overcome this habit completely, to breathe it away, to breathe it out of myself—or, rather, to veil it so that I could perceive things even more clearly. (So I reflected under the chestnut trees outside the Pazin station, remembering the beautiful night in the hotel and the first rays of sun on the window frame.) Now the noise—yes, noise—of the pigeons high in the trees, like the sound of conversations below, became decisive, urgent, as if up in the treetops they believed themselves unique. From the trees dropped a snowfall of small white feathers. With a hoarse caw, one of the pigeons flew down and minced around the station square before fluttering majestically straight back up into the leaves, its feathers whispering like a shaken sack of straw. The pigeons were very light in color with a dark, emblematic stripe on their tailfeathers. Their dainty heads were even a shade lighter. They were convinced they were unique. Where were Pazin's sparrows? I watched a circle of them whirl up from the dust—a seventh-day creation. Nearby, a pigeon, with a bobbing head and a piece of straw in its beak, left the sparrows' realm suddenly and was soon just a shadow in the sunny foliage. Large and small flies, previously unnoticed on the sticky oil-cloth in the station buffet, were lapping up spilled drops.

Were those flocks of birds in the crannies of the sink-hole walls also pigeons, illuminating its depths with their bright wings? Similarly, a single white butterfly's wobbling search for its mate intensified the green darkness under the chestnut trees. Meanwhile, waiting passengers (who had become quite numerous) stood around under the pigeons' din like a collection of unnecessary things.

So I have decided to skip my train and to stay in Pazin with Sunday's pigeons. Then occurred the first of that day's so typically Yugoslavian coinci-dences: I saw a child with a white eye-patch—the train to Pula has arrived—just as, *simili modo*, last night I saw a slender young girl wearing a bright frayed bandage on her knee, a bandage that seemed almost a decoration because of its fringes and the charming way the girl straightened her knee. (The train to Pula has departed.) And I also noticed the station's pillars, here in Pazin, slender, round and fluted in the old Austrian style. A small flag pole stuck out of the cornice under the enormous main capital. The sparrows had become barely visible, mere whistling shadows over the asphalt. The train to Dirska pulled in, the one I had previously planned on taking. Passengers scrambled to the train's doors despite its having stopped. Soon, this train too had gone, leaving behind only one woman in a black dress with a white aster on her purse. The pigeons, momentarily quiet, now hesitantly began, one at a time, to echo the train's whistle. I took my time, of which I had plenty.

Many of Pazin's houses still bear traces of the original gables. The former trapezoids of these Istrian houses—squares topped with triangles—have been expanded and filled in to form rectangles. Meanwhile, the pigeons with their dark, guttural cooing completely blanketed the entire town; and the many holes in the railroad worker's blue shirt turned out merely to be groups of flies, which were doubtless squatting all over my back as well; wasps, burrowing in the garbage, scared off whirls of the flies. My head ached from seeing and hearing so much. One pigeon, just landed, let its dark pinions hang down from the lighter colored feathers of one wing as it circled and pecked, and then let the pinions hang from the other wing, looking like some kind of amphibious vehicle—then it hopped down into the gutter. The back of its neck gleamed quite brightly as it flew up into the station's canopy. Nothing airier than the wafting breezes, I thought. And then, in the noonday stillness, all the roosters in this small town began to crow at once. A cat slunk into the station square, and although small, began stalking the flighty birds like a lion. In the alley leading down to the sink-hole was a rooster with a glowworm in its beak. I freed the glowworm which sat stunned a while before finally raising its head. In a garden near the hole, a turkey in a wire cage raised its head in the same way. Then, finally, near the sea on this Sunday evening, a palm frond shuddered like a thousand birds.

SHEET-LIGHTNING EPOPEE
OR
ONCE AGAIN FOR THUCYDIDES

On November 24, 1987, flares of sheet-lightning in the sky ("the stars' eyes" as the ancient Greeks called it) wandered over the Yugoslavian island Krk, across the entire horizon, blaze after blaze, as if each flare were answering the previous one. These flares were of very different sizes and kinds: first, light would cover the entire firmament with its silent flash, raise from the darkness cloud formations that were otherwise sunk in the night, and serrate the tip of the island out of its invisibility on the ground below; then, a tiny flicker would bring out only the contour of a cloud fragment; then, nothing more than a weak sputter of light from behind shapeless clouds; and once again, a silent, all-encompassing flash, a soundless whirring from the zenith down to the last few men out on the village streets, where the electric wires had hummed in the calm before the storm and the last small red and yellow autumn leaves—acacia fans, parched, crumbling in mid-flight—now flew through the flash. Finally a tremendous noise, the rolling of thunder, sounded behind the crests of mountains and waves, for a time followed only by wan, silent, but extensive flashes. At last, unexpectedly, in the midst of a flash scattered across the sky, the first tree of lightning appeared, its branches shining with the sheet-lightning. Abruptly, and from all directions, both lightning bolts and sheet-lightning blazed. In the next moment a storm tide rushed into the port. Towering waves crashed against the doors of the pier houses. Although the observer fled all the way back to the farthest part of the harbor, the spray surged up over his hips as he took the last steps to his lodgings. Deeply moved, the wet man entered the hotel whose plinth was already covered by the surf. He awoke late that night to the richest of star-filled skies, under which, however, sheet-lightning had again begun to flash, rising up to the seven stars of the Pleiades and the quietly glowing twins, Castor and Pollux. The tips of the flashes now reached down below the low-lying fringes of the clouds over the sea, once again calm, and up to the very edges of the constellations. And yet, they did not extinguish the stars, but instead exposed them even more clearly as pictures. This was the sheet-lightning over the Yugoslavian island Krk on the night from the 24th to the 25th of November, 1987.

THE SHOESHINE MAN OF SPLIT

After he had gazed for a long time, on December 1, 1987, at the carved figures on the wooden door of the cathedral in Split, with St. John at the Last Supper again laying his head on Jesus' shoulder but this time seeking consolation with one hand on his master's sleeve, the traveler descended to the sunny beach promenade where he saw an aged shoeshine man. The traveler watched him, certainly idle for some time, begin to shine his own shoes. And they needed it.

He shined them as carefully as if they were a customer's; in fact he couldn't have done otherwise: slowly, carefully, one piece of leather at a time. And his shoes, gently caressed, began to gleam and finally shone under the palm tree where the shoeshine man sat. "Well then, I'll also go and have him shine my shoes!" thought the traveler. And so he did. The shoeshine man used even the crooked brush with a gentleness and, at the same time, a firmness that comforted the feet, the instep, the ends of the toes. In his shoe polish tin, only a small lump the size of a fingernail remained, but with it he managed to polish, swab by swab, gradually, completely, deeply, all surfaces of both ankle boots. He handled each flake of polish with care, never using two on the same spot. At last he even turned the lid over, hoping to find yet another trace of polish there. He tightened the traveler's shoelaces, very slowly and evenly, with an almost festive grip, and stuck them between the necks of the boots and socks. (The shoeshine man's own socks hung down. Long underwear, darkened at the hem, peeked out from under his trousers; likewise, above, the completely blackened shirt-collar seemed something entirely independent or self-sufficient.) When he took up the two polishing brushes and alternately rushed them over each of the shoes, his work became a performance. The sweep of the brushes cut through the tumult of the port promenade as a very soft, rustling, delightful music, the sweeping of a jazz drummer listening to his music with a particularly deep concentration, no, finer still, more delicate, more urgent, the unexpected power of the muezzin's call to prayer from atop the minaret. The · dark berries, fallen from the palm trees into puddles left by the afternoon's winter rain, formed a large archipelago that shone in the sun.

Above them swayed the shoeshine man's round head with the white crown of hair and the tanned scalp. Each time the traveler put the other foot forward, the old man rapped hard and swiftly on his crate with one of the small brushes, made, it seemed, just for this purpose. The shoes gleamed as they never had before, but, with his small, black cloth, the man reached his finale. He first shook out his little rag in a miniature ceremony and then, for his coda, stroked the toe-caps—and only them—so that, from the smallest, only now visible, wrinkles and scratches in the leather, they emitted a final, additional shimmer that had never seemed possible. Then, finished with his work, he tapped curtly. As the traveler left, he was more pleased than he'd ever been with the shine of the shoes on his feet. In the restaurant, he pulled his legs in under the table so that no one would brush against them and perhaps dirty them accidentally. Even later, on the bus, he kept his feet just in front of his seat, avoiding any carelessness in the aisle, making sure that no new passengers even came near his shoes. In the middle of the shoeshiner's performance, he had had the impression that this man was his portrait-painter, completely different from the painters of tourists he'd recently seen—incomparably more fitting, truer, better suited to the traveler. In the shoeshine man of Split he briefly saw a saint: the saint of carefulness, or the "Saint of Small Measures." Days later, when it was raining, further south, he left his shoes in his room. The following week, however, he wore them in the snow of Macedonia, in the coal dust of the Peloponnesian mountains, in the yellow and gray sands of the Libyan and Egyptian deserts. And even months later, one day in Japan, he needed only to rub the cloth briefly over the leather, and the original gleam of the promenade of Split reappeared, undiminished.

EPOPEE OF LOADING A
CARGO SHIP

When he arrived, on December 5, 1987, at the pier of the Dubrovnik port, about one hour before the ferry's departure to the islands, there stood against the wall some very carefully constructed window shutters, doors just as carefully crafted, with locks but still without keys, and several stacks of small red tiles bound together with iron bands. Some men stacked wooden beams of various widths and lengths from an overloaded truck onto the boat's afterdeck. In front, in the bow, a number of passengers were already seated in the large, glass-walled cabin below, and an uninterrupted stream of additional passengers from the city boarded with their purchases for the islands: sacks of potatoes, gas containers, replacement parts for machines, televisions, oil cans, and empty cans without lids, plastic bags filled with fruit, eggs, laundry detergent. Some also carried great heavy trunks. One woman appeared with a bouquet of very long-stemmed red carnations. She reminded the onlooker of another woman who, several days earlier in Split, returned from a different island, holding a more varied bouquet of its many-colored, small wildflowers. Once the wooden beams were finally stowed away, an older worker loaded the tiles with a forklift, one stack after the other, onto the back of the boat. He first lifted the tiles gently onto a wooden grate and then lifted them together onto the boat deck, where other workers shoved another, rolling grate underneath. Each time, the heavy load landed softly, with great precision, and then was rolled away by several young men who appeared at once powerful and gentle, pushing from behind to a spot that had, earlier, been exactly delineated. The hold meanwhile was almost full. The last load fit within a hair's breadth, with no room to spare, in the very last niche. Nothing, not a single man or object, was even scratched during the difficult and lengthy manoeuvre. Even the smallest procedure, up to the closing of the railing, was completed without hesitation, clearly, deliberately, and overlapped into the next. The entire loading of the parts of the house occurred calmly, at least without noise and shouts and haste. The passengers now sat outside in the sun, in front and on the upper deck, among them a serious young woman with one arm stretched out behind her on the back of her seat, the other forward on her knee, her head raised, gazing at the distance. The repeated signal of departure was so loud that it echoed off the hills on one side and the highrises of the peninsula on the other. The assembled, pale faces of the childlike sailors! The onlooker almost waved to the young woman. She would have waved back. It was the setting for a Hamsun novel: the pier of a Norwegian fjord with a trading center at the turn of the century. But how much more beautiful, real, and expansive that the scenery should unfold over the hour without being contained in a novel. Then the forklift disappeared with the old man. Spewing black smoke, the boat steamed rapidly toward the islands, a five-pointed partisan star on its smoke-stack. Only one person was left on the pier. No one else was there to see off any passengers or the material for the island house well on its way. In the sky, blue above the noon emptiness, a seagull hung in the wind, bobbing its head. Below, a flock of sparrows in the recently formed puddle, their number caught at first glance. These were the events on the Dubrovnik/Dalmatia pier between noon and one o'clock on December 5, 1987.

THE TALE OF HATS IN SKOPJE

A possible brief epic: the different hats passing by in large cities. For example, in Skopje in Yugoslavian Macedonia on the tenth of December, 1987. Even in the middle of this city, there were those *passe-montagne* or mountain climbing hats that cover the nose as well as the forehead, leaving only the eyes free. The small black skullcaps of the cart drivers passed among them, while on the sidewalk an old man, wearing a hood covered with pointed gables like those on Islamic windows and pillars, said goodbye to his daughter or granddaughter from Titograd, Montenegro, or Vipava, Slovenia (the daughter or granddaughter was crying). The snow melted as it fell in southernmost Yugoslavia. And then a kepi embroidered with a white oriental pattern passed under the dripping snow, followed by a blond girl in a thick, bright ski hat (with a tassel on top), and right after her came a man wearing glasses and a beret with a dark blue stem. A soldier's beret followed, then police hats in pairs with visors and lightly indented tops. Surrounded by a flock of women in black veils, one man went by in a fur hat with the earflaps tied up. Then a man wearing a fez pulled down over his ears and spotted black and white like a magpie—the dappled Feirefiz, Parzival's halfbrother. His companion wore a hat of fur and leather and behind them came a child with a black and white headband. Another man, looking like a black marketeer in his salt-and-pepper hat, darted through the slush-covered Macedonian bazaar street. Then troops of soldiers marched by with the

Tito star adorning the front of their caps. Next came someone with a brown loden Tyrolean hat, the front brim bent down and the back standing straight up, a silver badge on its side. Young girls traipsing by in suede hoods with lining; a light gray shepherd's hat tied down with a red strap; a heavy-set woman in a white linen chef's hat that was fraying in back. A young man with an intricately constructed leather cap, each panel a different color. One man pushed a cart wearing a plastic hat over his ears and a Palestinian shawl over his chin. Then another went by with a rose pattern on his hat, while bareheaded passersby also appeared occasionally, with their own hair as headwear. A child, carried, in a stocking cap, passed by a woman with a wide brimmed hat set at a sweeping angle: it was impossible to keep up with the variety. A beautiful woman with glasses and a lilac Borsalino hat sauntered by and turned the corner, followed by a very small woman with a hand-knit hat which rose up high on her head, followed by an infant in an open-crowned sombrero, carried by a young woman in an especially large beret that read

Made in Hong Kong. A young man with a scarf over his ears and around his neck. A boy with skier's earmuffs, the brand: TRICOT. And so forth. A beautiful procession, so on and so forth.

CALLING THE ESCAPED PARAKEET IN PATRAS, PELOPONNESIA, ON DECEMBER 20, 1987

Today, Sunday, a man stood on a large flight of outdoor steps in the upper section of Patras with an open cage upon his head. An apple was impaled on the cage's spire. The man alternately spun the apple on the spire and threw it in the air, or, facing the top of the stairs, he pulled the bowl out of the cage, licked it expressively and raised it up to the trees, like a chalice, constantly calling "Malla!" ("Apple"?) for the missing bird. But only sparrows flew down from the branches and the last autumn leaves fluttered to the ground. The man constantly changed places with a farmer, spun the apple in his hand, spun it on top of the cage where it was skewered upon the spire, or needle. And so the birdcatcher's soft, continuous, never impatient call reigned over the acropolis stairs in Patras—"apple" is "melon" in Greek—as all around friends and neighbors constantly offered advice. In the meantime, the man drew back from the birdcage, which he had set down on one of the steps, and tried to lure the bird with silence, moving away from the escaped pet (papagallos), which had now hidden itself even deeper among the tree branches. Time and again the bird made noises or spoke while the traffic's muffled roar rose from the city center. Yet, for the most part, the man tried to entice the bird with the open cage on his head and the apple on top of the cage. It was a reddish-yellow apple and I believed it would have helped if the stem were not bent to the side, but stood straight up, pointing to the bird in the tree. The papagallos sat high up in the tree, beyond the reach of a normal ladder. And when I arrived in Olympia late that evening (accompanied from the central train station to the dubious hotel, as I had been throughout my entire trip, or at least since Dubrovnik, by the same silent, melancholy, spotted dog—in fact, in Olympia I was escorted through the Peloponnesian twilight and right into the cold hotel by two of these cringers), I wondered if the man on the darkened acropolis steps in Patras was still calling his parakeet, wearing the cage or the apple, or both, on his head. Once, and only once, as he juggled the fruit did it fall to the ground. And the bird, hidden high up in the tree, answered the man as softly as the man's own call, but still did not show himself at all.

Several Incidents of
Snowfall in Japan

O n the evening of March 4, 1988, in the
Aomori seaport at the northern end of
Japan's main island, it finally began to
snow for the first time in the traveler's winter. (That
is, he had seen snow lying on the ground here and
there: on a snow-covered field in an undeveloped
no-man's land or *terrain vague*, rare for the
Japanese who let nothing go to waste, and on the
ground of a softly seething bamboo grove on
Morioka in middle Japan. He had even seen a

bridge of frozen snow over a black winter stream in a sparsely inhabited northern province. And yet, he had not once seen snow falling, much less felt the flakes on his face, on his temples, or, where they were most noticeable, on the groove from his nose to his upper lip.) An entire migration of flakes drifted in the darkness over the sea of Hokkaido and appeared black in the open hatchway of the ferry, which—as the underwater tunnel between the main and the adjacent islands would be opened the following week—was making one of its final runs. The next morning, the spaces between the houses—earthquake precautions—were almost completely filled. The trees grew out of the mountains of snow as though rooted to cliffs, but a neon sign in Japanese on a glass roof shone through even the thickest layers. With the heavy snow, the traveler now understood why the telephone booths in this city were elevated with stairs leading up to them. He put a chunk in his mouth and felt it tighten with the shock of the cold. The soft white snow-light shone again over Hokkaido. Behind the snow-dunes by the sea, tall poles rose up, swaying side to side and back and forth. They were mooring poles. The next morning, the first flakes fell in pairs, colliding and scattering. The snow continued to fall during the entire train ride inland with a delicateness that could almost have only been Japanese—the sheaves and stacks of rice grasses on the deserted fields seemed to belong to the snow. Flakes of the same shape and size spun around upon themselves, falling slowly and at apparently equal intervals past the cypresses and onto the rice paddies with empty causeways, past Hachinohe, onto Japan's vineyards. A single world of snowflakes spindled slowly on the breezes over the entire land. In the distance, especially near the dark forest edges, it fell wildly, as it did right at the train window. Only in the middle ground, where it was most easily discerned, did it fall with an almost primordial slowness: there on the rails of an empty Japanese village station (through which the train accelerated as if avoiding an ambush); and there on the blackish stream of a winter river bordered with icy snow; and also on the grassy embankment of a pale, snowless section of the rice paddy; on those poles that form a sculpture straining towards the sky; on the finely jointed Japanese reeds; on snow piles in the Sannohe train station; slithering and splintering soundlessly on the asphalt platform here (the name of the station indecipherable); spindling down to the ground from the clouds like countless coordinated trapeze artists, now falling on the wet and dry spotted highway; and on the tiny cemetery in the midst of a rolling field—small stones, like boundary stones, grouped around a single cypress—landing in the ring below and immediately disappearing, making room for the next ones. The flakes were shaped like Japanese written characters, characters that in turn produce names of Japanese places, Aomori, Hachinohe, Sannohe, Morioka and now Sendai. And the next day in the city of Matsushima on the eastern sea, the snow sank onto a section of fresh, smoking tar. In a moment, black became white. White and white turned into black and black—and the memory of the small animals that shrivel immediately when peasant children place them on a hot stove and of a book entitled *Snow on a Hot Bread Board*.

LAST PICTURES?

And yet were there still more pictures? Yesterday, March 30, 1988, in the La Coruña wineshop in Galicia, Spain, the children sitting between the casks at the back of the room kept looking up at the television while conscientiously doing their homework. Or the day before yesterday, in Vigo, on the Atlantic Ocean, there was a kind of marriage of river and ocean waves: one did not incorporate the other, but rather, there in the estuary, incredibly gently with a light snapping sound, one was dissolved into and extinguished by the other. The river's murmur met the tide's rush and, with a stronger murmur, the river and ocean waves joined and streamed out into the ocean. It was strange how the ocean waves crept first to the edge of the river's mouth and then, with the ebb and flow, stole into the land's interior. The sea's waves had seemed more powerful, but in the center of the estuary, the river's waves were in fact much stronger. At the moment the two streams flowed or sailed by one another, a peculiar hissing came from the sea detritus, the alluvial sand, and the crackling mussel shells piled up by the river's stream. At the exact threshold dividing river and ocean there was a striking underwater turbulence—colliding, churning clouds of mud, and a powerful welling up of silver sand (Galicia is a land of granite) with billions of rock splinters briefly thrown up and catching the sunlight—a kind of curtain drawn between the two realms, a glittering gloom of tide rip between river and ocean, a changing of the guard. The ocean surged upstream into the river, then together they flowed into the salty tide water, and the river's bubbling met the sea's roar so that it was drowned out like the chirping of sparrows by rushhour traffic.

And a few days earlier, at the beginning of Holy Week, another of these "final" pictures in Santiago de Compostela, also in Galicia. For hours on end, one provincial priest after another came to one of the cathedral's side chapels with a triune flask and pouch, in order to collect his church's yearly ration of oil from three enormous casks: unction, holy oil, chrism. With a long-handled ladle, a cathedral priest poured each portion into the bronze, silver, or leaden flasks—the latter being those of the poorest parishes. After screwing on lids and closing up their pouches, the priests then wiped their fingers on a specially prepared towel. The thick, glossy Galician olive oil with yellowish-green streaks had a strong aroma, no, fragrance. I imagined one of the priests, many of whom were shorn, going straight through town and across the steppe with the newly consecrated oil in his threefold pouch, to a remote, deserted military chapel where he lit the eternal light with this oil. I imagined another, without clerical garb, as the lover of a pale young woman, who—nervously, smiling, yet open, sexual—waited in the nave, away from the large casks. ("Good Luck!") At this point I recognized the bearded, large young priest dispensing the oil as the one who had officiated the morning mass, laying the Host upon the pilgrims' hands or outstretched tongues whereupon his thumbs clearly had been bitten several times. Now he was standing behind a plastic-covered table in back of the three enormous containers and, with dripping ladle in hand, he waited for the next priest to come and collect the oil. In the meantime, those parish priests who had already been served had set their canisters down in every corner. They lingered a while and chatted. " 'Til next year's consecration."

THE GLOWWORM EPOPEE

One epopee is still missing (no, many are still missing): that of the glowworms. How, for example, they were "suddenly there," not glowing but blinking, on the path through the fields between Cormons and the village of Brazzano in Friuli, last night, from the 29th to the 30th of May, 1988—the way they sat on the path, illuminating the ground with their glowing bodies, or blinked like airplanes among the tall grasses. On the palm of the night stroller's hand one lit up the lines, a long glow just next to his life-line. From up close it appeared as if light, luminous tractors were strapped onto the small, dark crea-tures. Then, when he looked up, the bugs' flashes across the entire Friulian plain glowed brighter than the stars above, as if it were the first hour of the glowworms' appearance this year, the celebra-tion of their reappearance in the world. Ah, this epopee should be so much more compelling and should tell more exactly how a group of these crea-tures sat in the crannies of the path's surface and, with their constant flashing, illuminated a runway upon which their fellows could silently land; how, when taken in the palm of my hand, they did not stop glowing, but glowed even brighter; how there, in my hand, the flashing became a constant, peace-ful glow; and how I just now opened my other hand in an attempt to reenact the events of that night as I wrote them down; it should tell how I spoke with them, how I blew on them, as though trying to get them to glow more—and, as I imag-ined—they did. I also imagined that the glowing section was warm and even gradually became red-hot, burning my hand (however, now in daylight, there is unfortunately no scar). This epopee should tell how I started at the thought that a glowing thing was sitting right on my life-line and could burn it up. But no, it was sitting on the line next to it, the one I believed was my "luck-line." It should tell how, when I held the creature lightly between my thumb and forefinger in an invitation to fly off into the darkness, it lit up my fingerprints as labyrinthine shapes in the night; how these glowing creatures, rising higher and higher, flew through the branches of the apple and cherry trees, giving these nocturnal trees and the developing, ripening fruit their particular and unexpectedly soft night shapes; how—as the lit train to Trieste passed by in the distance and the worms seemed to glitter all the more forcefully—I naturally imagined, after a laborious, barren day, a god had given me back a design, this small, blessed, glittering design, branching out deep into the night, of the vacillating, tiny newborn glow-worms that are often found floating over the

Friulian plain, a plain that gradually grows to enormous dimensions around them. This mobile design that (think of Pasolini's "despairing emptiness of Casarsa") restored my soul after the laborious, barren day. And that, finally, would be the little epic of the glowworms on the night from the 29th to the 30th of May, 1988, between the town of Cormons and the village of Brazzano in Friuli.

Brazzano Thunder Blues

ontinuous thunder just now, on June 18, 1988, among the Friulian clouds constant-· ly wandering across the sky. The rumbling breaks out suddenly, then, just as suddenly, softens into a distant grumble higher up in a dark cloudbank. For a long time, the rumbling has not let up for even a moment on this spring afternoon: now a sudden spate of bombs exploding, now the flapping of a bedsheet, now a great palaver and racket, now the fall of a bowling pin. I had never heard thunder go on for this long: the strange, ceaseless murmur of a crowd up above, not quite reminiscent of gods' gossiping. And, in fact, it still does not stop and does not stop. It simultaneously does and does not wish to end. From one ear to the other, the thunder rattles between horizons, across the entire sky, alternating with flashes of lightning that seem to rekindle it and goad it on whenever it dies down to a simple murmur. To me, this thunder is an old man in his enormous house—the open sky above—complaining, implacable, announcing to those on the ground that he will not let them disperse until he has had his say: "Now I'm talking and this will take a while." He does not relent for a moment but grumbles again as soon as the thunder appears to recede to neighboring skies.

And now, for an entire hour already, the thunder's constant nattering and grousing, roaring and crackling, bursting and muttering and grumbling throughout the sky, called up again and again from the lightning's afternoon dozes, whereupon the old, blustering voice rises up and tumbles out in all directions, tired, but duty-bound. It is a shame, actually, that this seemingly endless talking at my head must end at some point, for a simple rainstorm will eventually take its place in my ears that now need—are even addicted to—this thunder or thunderer. But now, for one moment more, thank heavens for a new flash and a freshly invigorated clap of thunder, and yet again, as the chairs on the pizzeria's wooden terrace sway in the rainstorm and the curtains inside float in the afternoon quiet. The wind blows under my arms now that I have finished my afternoon's work. At the same time, the thunder rolls here and there, back and forth, across the open landscape, as if shot from cannons, continuously for almost two hours now. Or was it the flaring of a bonfire on the southern hill and now one on the northern hill? Or is it actually fusillades in the vineyards within and beyond the Yugoslavian border?

Clatter on thunder. Mutter, rumble, rattle, grind, rasp, grouse, grumble, crack, and roar your thunder-blues—the longest clap of thunder that ever swelled over the earth. But no, now there are in fact fusillades aimed against you in the sky while above and below all is caught up in an increasingly abrupt battle with sallies and retreats: a battle fought down below as if over this year's vintage. Ah, thunder—if only it were just your extended celestial rhythm and blues.

Again a Story of Melting

It was the 17th of February, 1989, in Llivia, a
Spanish enclave in the middle of the far
Pyrenean highlands called La Cerdaña. The bare
trees were draped with shreds from forest fires, and
there must have recently been a storm in the area:
all the leaves of past years were piled up in banks on
the sides of the houses and roads. At the fences, the
cows grazed busily, the hair on their necks fur-
rowed by the barbed wire. A stillness descended, as
is still possible even in this century—but only in

solitude? A frozen spring appeared on the edge of the pasture, under the midday sun of the highlands. Below the ice a clear bubble with shining, supple edges wound in and around the same spot. As the ice gradually melted—an hour of watching passed in an instant—more and more small bubbles formed, pushing up from the depths against the thick frozen surface, promiscuous, and round, quickly floating away. Underneath, dark leaves whirled over the stream-bed. Just before the sheet of ice melted, one large bubble became frothy and ready to spawn. It formed many small bubbles, shifting from side to side; the entire bubble population, both large and small, was crowded together, set to go, each for itself, but for the moment the crowd continued to mill about and follow each other's leads. Small birds with sunset-red heads whirred by above this commotion. At the moment of liberation and their sailing away into the melting ice, the many small bubbles joined together in one shot, creating a new, large bubble, around whose edges, again, several small bubbles gathered, and so on, until the bursting of bubbles was widespread, and the entire spring bubbled, clear only at its very source, as the afternoon bells of Llivia tolled. Where the stream's ice was still solid, it retained the form of the grooves and peaks of leaves that had been washed or blown away, or frozen in the ice. The birds whirred by unafraid, very close, behind and in front of the seated observer, playing with him and with their own zigzagging shadows on the ice, while the sexes of the alders, at eye level, only gradually became evident: the male catkins, black, long, closed, and as if armaments, bomb-shaped (slender bombs), usually in groups of four, aimed at the much less numerous, light brown, open female "fruit-baskets," the latter usually grouped in little crowns of two or three, bobbing on much more fragile stems. In the meantime, below, under the strengthening sun, the still-frozen sheet of ice had taken on ever more reliefs of leaves, stems, and lances. Only near the granite post in the stream's center was it still smooth and solid, and only now did it begin to turn grainy. The distant sierra appeared hazy, the only smoke except for that of the fire in the field below, as if there were a snowstorm up on the crests of the Pyrenees in the broadly terraced Sierra del Cadí. Also, in the meantime, next to my bare feet, a clear bubble shaped like a horse's hoof wound in and around the same spot in the solid ice near the sparkling granite post. One half of it suddenly sped downstream. Without bubbles or foam or dividing itself, it soon disappeared, escaping into the spring water, free of ice, running very quietly, very quickly down to the Rio Segre which crossed the enclave and would let this water, newly freed from its cork of ice, stream into the Ebro and the Mediterranean . . . when? Meanwhile, the remaining bubble-half danced in the stream's ice which was, moment by moment, peeling off layers in the sun's warmth: a majorette-like dancing in place. I knew then that fulfillment—or, the right things—consisted of such hours. Yet, if I had had to stand before someone and portray it, I would have had nothing to say. I stuck my feet in the freshly melted stream of Llivia and thought, "Up and onwards!"

The Hour Between Swallows and Bats

I had always wanted to focus solely on, to experience completely, that time in the early evening after the last swallows have flown away and before the first bats arrive. And at least once, I wanted to see the very first bat appear in the twilight, like the evening star's first gleam. I had always missed the first bat's appearance, as well as the first star's. And just as I always noticed the evening star unexpectedly, after it had been visible for some time, when I set out to find the evening bats—even as early as an

hour before sunset—several of these twilight crea-
tures appeared suddenly among the swallows.

But my hour alone with the swallows and bats
did eventually occur. On March 24, 1989, in
Linares, in the mountains of northern Andalusia,
on a Good Friday, after a night of continual drum-
rolls from the Lenten processions throughout the
city and a day of writing alone out in the savannah
in the broken shade of a eucalyptus grove, I decided
to avoid any more drumming, and, sitting in an old
dumping ground, surrounded by stones and weeds,
I resolved: "I will stay until the bats come!"

At first, there were only swallows—for some
time there had only been swallows in the otherwise
empty sky above this no-man's land. And when the
first bat finally appeared, it fluttered over the small
blue campion-like flowers amidst the rubble, as if
greeting them, and I recalled the cuckoo's cry that
sounded all day over the steppe, and a squeaking, as
well as the now familiar moment each day when an
eagle's shadow would flit over my writing paper.

The bats came on like a soccer team warming

up for a game while the swallows set out over the fields, as if the one team were making way for the next and the initial bat had come to announce the change. The first few bats were still practicing—their game had not yet begun—as the drum-roll from the Good Friday procession continued. And in the meantime, their playing field—the sky over the dumping ground—was completely empty, finally empty of swallows but not yet taken over by the bats still preparing their entry. The sky was empty, but filled with expectation. Here and there a bat whizzed by across the playing field in short, rapid zigzags, as if teasing the audience and heightening the tension. A few last swallows returned yet again as if from far away and searching for something left behind, while the sparrows chirped ever more softly and the drumming from the now invisible city of Linares swelled up, only to be transcended at nightfall by a woman's voice singing an ecstatic dirge. High above it all floated an Arabic threnody, to which the bats, now out in full force, drew their sharply bent lines across the darkening sky.

Two Days Facing the
Cloud-Kitchen Mountain

Three days ago, on July 5, 1989, alone on a Sunday morning and surrounded by silence, I sat on the terrace of a house in the Salzburg Leopoldskroner moor, looking south at the Untersberg massif in the near distance with its stocky, pyramid-shaped summit almost six-thousand feet high. I watched for hours as the clouds emerged from the rock face, the slopes of gravel, and the crevices. The clouds puffed out of the mountain as if it were a single, enormous cloud-kitchen, first with its cooking area in the thicket of dwarf pines in dolinas hidden from my view, then with its cooking niche on the sheer face of limestone, emitting mist and vapor from its fissures, crevices, pits, and excavations, or, in a cooking frenzy, over the entire face of the mountain, using the last remains of the visibly melting snow as water. The clouds that the mountain continuously spewed out constantly changed their shape and color: first white, rising up volcano-yellow or red, then tapering and—on this rainy, spacious day—turning sky-gray. In the meantime, however, the mountain's cloud-kitchen remained immobile, stable, cooking up its clouds on the premises, so to speak, where they then settled, growing mostly in firmness, mass, thickness, and weight, primarily in the hourglass-shaped syncline of the bright cirque. Suddenly, movement was restored to this oppressive mass, which scattered rapidly as though bellows had been turned on it, in an abrupt ventilation. The clouds fled up to the rain-darkened peak and out into the distance over the gaps of the mountain passes, over towards Bavaria, down to Markt Schellenberg. A chain of elongated cloud commuter trains suited to the mountain gaps emerged, several of them in the slow-lane as it were or careening off into the open air, thinning out, floating downwards—into the chasms and ravines, to the north, towards me, the observer. They dispersed then sailed westward far from the mountainsides in the most diverse shapes, mostly of birds, eagles, hawks, seagulls, but also of flying lions, goats—chimerae!

That was three days ago, and today, in the middle of the week, on a florid, blue day in the heat of summer, I sit again on the terrace facing the Untersberg or Taigetos or Pindus, while the noise of the work day impinges on my view, fruitfully impeding (or grounding?) the act of pure contemplation. The mountain stood for a very long time without producing any clouds, empty, out of commission. The sloping hourglass of the cirque, usually the main site of cloud production, seemed shut down, cooled off, dried out, deserted. The sky-high cliff-sides appeared marmoreal, sealed. The entire verdant massif seemed completely and permanently clear, as dead to clouds as an extinguished furnace—during hours of waiting, the observer was thrown back upon his memory. Then, all at once, under a bright sky, the walls began to puff and smoke, and before my eyes cloud fragments poured like autumn smoke out of all the cracks and pores of the honeycombed, pitted mountain. They gathered together into a great family of clouds that shrouded the pyramidal peak, giving the edges a glowing trimming. Then, like the columns of smoke in the rice paddies of Hiroshige's woodcuts in nineteenth-century Japan, they climbed vertically over the farthest peak, and stood over the massif in the otherwise cloudless blue, as open to me as I to them. Out of the cirque's lava-fields, among them those of Untersberg-Etna, a steady supply of clouds rose from the fissures, the burners of the cloud-kitchen stove: white, lilac, rose, exactly the shade of the roses here, near the terrace balustrade, that sway lightly back and forth in the rising summer afternoon wind so that the shadows in the opening blooms grow larger and smaller. Now one of the roses is completely darkened for a moment from the inside out, while the house's shining black Labrador lies, massive, at my feet and pushes his nostrils here and there, and the concrete mixers, unnoticed by me, have been turned off for the lunch hour. In the distance, veils spin themselves out of the summit wall, lilac veils, spreading themselves evenly in all directions over the blue rock and, in all honesty, into the shapes of roses—or, even more beautiful, rosettes, at least for the duration of my moment. And now I will go and call my child.

ATTEMPT TO EXORCISE ONE
STORY WITH ANOTHER

I t was a Sunday, the morning of July 25, 1989, in the Hotel Terminus next to the Lyon-Perrache train station, in a room that directly overlooked the tracks. Opposite and far away, the watery clear green of trees in a gap between the railroad wires and the buildings hinted at a river, the Saône, just before it joined the Rhône. Above it, the swallows banked in front of, and as if with, the white—shot through with sky-blue—of the waxing moon, which then, full of holes, slowly drifted away like a cloud. The railroad workers, each carrying a brief-case, went their separate ways across the large field of tracks, otherwise filled with Sunday emptiness, and descended the far stairs past a dainty, turn-of-the-century house with round windows on its upper floors and overgrown with Virginia creeper. They walked on to their rooming house, a large concrete building, with almost all of its curtains drawn. Above, the swallows executed twisting stunts and below, the *cheminots'* briefcase clasps and watchbands flashed as they sporadically crossed the tracks. The rumble of a cargo train came in a curve as if from a large sawmill. Some of the railroad men also carried plastic bags and all wore short-sleeved shirts without jackets. They usually went in pairs, though once in a while some were alone, and their coming and going over the S-shaped path crossing the tracks did not end. Each time the one who was sitting at his window looked down, glancing away from his paper at them and so traveling with them, another one bobbed across. The path, empty for just a few moments, was crossed only by sunshine, and in the sky also, for an instant, there were no swallows. Only then did the traveler realize that the Hotel Terminus in which he had just spent the night had served as Klaus Barbie's torture chamber during the war. The corridors were very long and winding, and there were double doors. Only the sparrows chirped outside, in hiding, and a white butterfly swayed above the *chemin des cheminots*. For a moment a Sunday afternoon stillness reigned, even over this enormous train station in which, for the time being, no trains moved. Only in the crack between some curtains as they closed was there movement. This great stillness and peace over the area lasted for some time, while a plane tree's leaves stirred as if from its very roots in front of the Virginia creeper house, and the white splinter of a gull twitched far away over the invisible river Saône, and the summer Sunday wind blew through the open room of the Hotel Terminus. And finally another worker began bobbing across the tracks, in short-sleeves, with a black briefcase held knee-high, sure of his goal—his free arm swinging. A small blue butterfly landed on one of the tracks, shining in the sun, and turned in a half circle as if moved by the heat, and the children of Izieux screamed to the heavens, almost a half century after their deportation, but only now as they should.

THE SHORT FABLE OF THE ASH TREE IN MUNICH

The ash tree stood (stands) in the middle of a public garden that is almost as large as a meadow and through which traffic roars. It is by far the largest tree there, in the center of Munich, and I had long been acquainted with it. Almost a decade ago I had shot arrows with friends at a target fastened to its trunk. Through the years, I would occasionally watch from home or from the garden, as the wind blew the leaves about arbitrarily or lifted the bare, supple branches with the crack of a whip. But on a day in late October, 1989, in the dark, clear light of an autumn storm, the tree stepped out of its usual role—which had in fact gradually become a cherished one—and unexpectedly became the site of an event. The site of an event? No, the ash itself changed (from an image) into an event. How did it begin? What happened first? First there was the color of the bark covering the very thick trunk that could perhaps have been encircled by the arms of two men and a child. When I happened to pass it on my usual walk through the garden before going home and sitting down at my desk, the vault of the sky in my field of vision unexpectedly began to shine despite the overcast day. The deep gray of the ash's bark, running to black in the wrinkles, seemed to glow, full of color. I approached the tree. The dark gray with its coal-black shimmer literally warmed my forehead and eyes. As I slowly circled the mammoth trunk, this color changed. The coal-gray merged—first in small, isolated islands, then in great tracts—with the yellowed white of the many lichens lining the wrinkles. This was followed by a strip of damp green moss rising straight up the trunk in a vertical central stripe and branching out at the fork into a virtual forest. I had probably already seen this dark green many times when passing by—but on this day the tree revealed its windward side as a singular occurrence. For this moment, the tree stood with its many colors both in the city center and, at the same time, self-sufficient, far outside it in the country. Where then? Karl Valentin's answer when asked where exactly a certain house stood is fitting: "Out in the open." Seen from Leopold Street, from the triumphal arch with its peculiar inscription, *Dedicated to victory—destroyed by war—admonishing peace*, the ash suddenly seemed transplanted into the wilderness. Its varying colors had pushed back the clamor of the adjacent street, and the most penetrating noise was the simmering of the leaves in a crown already grown thin. I had never been able to fix upon the cardinal points in Munich, a rather flat city with mountains only seldom visible on the horizon. But now, on the tree bark, these points were more obvious than on a compass or signpost. The zenith-line, so to speak, of the windward side, the West, would be there where the forest of moss shot up, and the other directions in the circle were established accordingly. The coal-gray section, whose changing colors began the story of this tree, faced east towards the central train station and further towards Austria, where I had just come from that afternoon. In the crevices, in the moss of the West—of the Rheinland, the Netherlands, the English Channel—all sorts of creatures were milling about: ants, moths, mayflies, winged beetles, each one scurrying up the trunk and concerned only with itself. I was gripped with excitement at knowing that if I slowly, continuously, circled and examined the tree, much more would be revealed. But since I was afraid of experiencing too much too quickly, I put it off until the next day. I stroked the bark's sharp ridges with my fingers as if to sharpen the sense of touch in my fingertips, and went into the house, to my desk.

On the next day the "garden hour" finally arrived. Throughout the entire morning I had looked forward to examining the tree, and now, before turning to it, I spent some time in the distance walking up and down and back and forth so that I would be clear-eyed and "breathing freely" for the observation. Then I slowly approached the bare, clear gray, east side of the trunk, riddled with deep, vertical grooves awaiting me at eye level. Once again I circled the massive tree whose curvature rotated as if I were revolving around a foreign planet in outer space. And again the planet altered its color and shape. The naked gray changed to the flat-white of the lichen and this in turn to the jungle-green of the moss shooting up the trunk. Yet something was no longer right between me and the tree. That is, the excitement of the day before was restored, but now it narrowed the scope of my focus and made my casual, selfless observation willful and overzealous. I did see a larger world again within the small one, but to do so, I was more than just looking. That larger world did not arise as effortlessly as it had the day before. Because I was approaching the tree for a second time, even if my gaze was not deliberate, I was perhaps too set on continuing and expanding the phenomenon of the tree. . . . Actually, there was really nothing deliberate in my perception of the little creatures in the bark's crevices as mountain climbers alone out in the wide world—one of them struggling up and around an overhang, another bivouacking in a niche on a cliff-face, a third swinging on a cable of spider's thread—and yet, all at once, with all the excitement of my observation, I felt as if I were committing an act of violence against the tree-phenomenon. Why the devil did I think of a thousand-year-old drop of amber at the sight of that ant's spherical, shining abdomen of a red verging on translucent yellow? Why did I see, against my will, the black dot inside the sphere as the famous fly preserved in amber? What difference did it make that I was transported through the thickly tangled arms of moss waving in the air to the impenetrable virgin forests of Japan, where all of a sudden, in a violent hallucination, my ears were filled with the chattering of bands of monkeys swinging in the treetops? With what validity or responsibility, when facing the anthracoid pattern of the bark, was I lifted above (or brought into) the immense bed of coals that appeared for a moment so ready to burst into flames that, thoroughly caught up in the illusion, I blew on it and believed I saw its edges and rims smoulder, glimmer, and gleam? I dropped to my heels on the grass and fallen leaves in front of the tree. The trunk, slightly wider at the base, thrust its roots, of which only the very beginnings were visible, directly into the earth. Just before it disappeared into the ground, the cracks of the bark ran together, branched out, fused with those of the adjacent pattern, formed diamond shapes unlike the pattern above, where the cracks ran almost parallel. And again, without my contriving it, this simple, meaningless picture was transformed, or rather, changed suddenly: instead of the rhomboid pattern on the roots, I saw the knotted Langobardic design that is chiseled, for example, into the early

Christian flagstones in Cividale in Friuli, whose knots, threads, and twists I had patiently traced. What I had experienced in the design as a whole-some testing of my patience, I now found in this transposed image, the tree bark as Langobardic knot ritual, to be no longer wholesome, almost annoying—and it was out of annoyance that I scolded myself when I stood up and looked away, trying to shake off the visual simile. Hadn't I always felt alienated or even repulsed when other writers used their sense of imagery in this way (in the work of Ernst Jünger, for instance, but also in that of the so much less pretentious Julien Green), parading their mystical gift for an omnipresence that could always transform a modern ruin into an ancient temple or change the calyx of a lily into an oriental king's tent out of whose depths the appropriate shawm music immediately resounds? And now (not for the first time—this had happened to me time and again), immersed as I was in my desire for the simple, unadorned validity of things, this frivolous-ness also fluttered within me as nothing other than suspicious displays of imagery, even before each session of writing. It began to rain. Single leaves, whole fans of leaves, and among them long, bare stems, fell from the ash above its trunk. The bark on which I rubbed my fingertips—this time so that it finally would be nothing but bark—smelled of the fires we used to build in a cow pasture under a similar ash tree and in similar autumn rain. Almost a decade ago I had closely observed just such an ash tree, also in early November. Like this tree, it was full of leaves in the morning, but dropped them quickly, one after the other, and stood with its branches bare in the noon light. The fans spun as they fell, crinkling, crackling, colliding. They each somewhat resembled a half-charred airplane falling into a spin. Once again, a leap to images. . . . I finally turned away from the tree, at least for today. In the farthest corner of the park stood a boxwood tree. A number of its tiny leaves were, as usual, round, and, while it rained softly upon the expanse of park, the water flowed in fits and starts out of these round leaves, whereupon the little chalices bounced upwards when emptied. Interspersed throughout the traffic noise were the southern Slavic voices of those looking at the secondhand cars lined up along the shoulder of the road. Between the enormous statue of a woman atop the triumphal arch and the dainty ones down in the garden there was a peculiar contrast—the muscular colossus above strode through the air with four similarly powerful lions on leashes while the fine-limbed women below, one leg in front of the other, fastened the shoulder straps on their dresses? Or, rather, untied them? I decided that on the following day, on my way through the park, I would make a wide detour around the mammoth ash in order to avoid any glimpse of it.

Days later, in a brilliant blue sky cleared by the Föhn and with a gentle breeze, the autumn sun shone sideways, almost horizontally, as if in a corner of the arctic, and the grass was newly green. I avoided the tree for a long time as I crisscrossed the park. For a time I could hear the falling leaves and the many-limbed stems, grating against the cracked trunk as they shot down like arrows, and the soft flapping of the thrushes as they flew through the garden. Then the din from the street took over: engines roaring, tires squealing, sirens howling. Indistinctness followed; and a lassitude that, along with the racket, weighed on my brain. As I turned towards the tree, I was tempted to approach it, to think something up for it, to ascribe something to it. And yet I could not see the tree as anything other than a refuge—and why shouldn't I? Approach the many-limbed figure without qualms and immerse yourself in it—just avoid the pull of the frieze of fluid images with which you pose as a sort of emperor of an alternate world. Take as a warning the example of the poet, Paul Claudel, who, in Japan on his solitary nature walks, compared himself to Caesar returning in triumph to Rome. The tree stood there, like nothing else, embodying only the present. It was no longer the central axis of the park, no eye-catcher, much less the "tree-world" it had been. The lamp-yellow sun brought out the bark's relief and the many little creatures there seemed both to toil for themselves and to work together. The ash was nothing other than merely present, and yet it was still extraordinary. Simply there, it was, nonetheless, still active—it reminded me of, or (why not use the old expression?) put me in mind of, what? Of nothing in particular. And, in addition, it taught, or better, told me (made it possible for me) to what?—to use what stood at head- and eye-level to measure the present that expanded before me.—It was All Soul's Day, November 2, 1989, and I tried to think of all the dead, the murdered, but I could not. All that occurred to me in the large park were the words "no-one's rose." Then a peacock butterfly landed suddenly on the one bush in the corner of the park still full of white flowers on this warm November day, as if a great many eyes were raised, lined with red. Next to them with its blue wings, the butterfly did in fact somewhat resemble a peacock. And finally, once again, as if I were its guardian, I circled the ash, which astounded me anew. I was astonished by the bark's manifold graying—its turning gray as well as blue and green—the color of a strange familiarity and friendship, and by the realm of light in the tree's crown (with a single raven perched at the very top). It awakened in me the desire to do something appropriate, to *be* in a manner befitting this light, this lightness, the leaves' permeability to the breezes, this mobility, these many fine limbs. I bent over the tall, naked blades of grass and threw them like arrows at the trunk, embedded in which I then found the rusted nail from the target of years ago.

In the afternoon, the much smaller ash trees in the English Garden, designated by a sign reading FRAXINUS EXCELSIOR; and later, just before evening, on Prinzregenten Strasse across the way, a look at a streetcar rail: sand, leaves, and pebbles, which for the moment belong in the story of the ash tree near the triumphal arch.

Epopee of the Disappearing Paths or Another Lesson of Mont Sainte-Victoire

FOR S.

Again on a return trip, slowly across Europe, he stopped in Aix-en-Provence in early January 1990, in order to reach Mont Sainte-Victoire. He had become sedentary for a time during his travels, immersed in his work in alien surroundings that challenged him daily and fruitfully. He now hungered for a return to one of the paths that had proven to bring him inspiration many times, where the earth was springy under his feet, where he was surrounded by green and the sky took on the old blue in all its former freshness. Having turned off the road outside of the city, and continued on to the trusted *chemin de Bibémus* from which one continues along the plateau path, and, after several hours, to the white mountain, he did in fact feel the desired stillness gradually returning to him. The measure of his step became a dance and set the rhythm for the rest. And again the peak of the distant Sainte-Victoire appeared at first glance to be an erratic block rising from the heather. Then, in a blind passage, the path led through the remains of a forest fire. He had often seen such devastation on his travels, each time as a more or less extensive firebreak after which the green, the smell of the pines, and the birdsongs resumed. But this time the firebreak did not end. Each small row of trees that appeared unharmed was followed by a larger strip of a black and gray landscape of coal and ashes. Only now did the traveler remember that in the previous summer he had heard of a forest fire on Sainte-Victoire without thinking it unusual. Forest fires are an integral part of summer here and would, in the immense area around the massif, jagged as it was, be rather occasional and inconspicuous. Admittedly, the one time that he had seen a forest burn with his own eyes it had been a terrifying sight. The fire storm had roared up the hill and the flames had sprung up repeatedly from the smoke-enshrouded trees so high that the air itself seemed to ignite and explode into balls of fire over the forest as it crashed to the ground. The tops of the pine trees were sprinkled about far away from the splintered trunks strewn around the silent burnt area. Many were stuck head-first in the layer of ashes that still smelled of burning. They recalled that moment when perhaps the storm, roaring in before the lustful flames, beheaded them.

On the path that passed ever more remains of trees and piles of dead underbrush, the traveler finally came upon a spot where both the whole area and the mountain could be seen at once. From the crest that was shimmering as it always had, down over the undercliffs on the plain, he saw that the fire had not simply burned a break through the vegetation. It had burned everything as far as the eye could see—and from this point one's vantage stretched as far as those in old landscape paintings—from the foothills, across the plateaux, to the last, solitary stunted bushes way up in the fissures of the otherwise bare cliff face. The mountain itself—not only the vegetation, but also the stone, the lime, the dolomite and marble—seemed consumed. It looked smaller and more formless. The spell of the magnificent Sainte-Victoire, the mountain of blessedness (because of the light, its colors, and the stillness), was broken by the fire. The mountain was denuded, stripped of its very last colored veil, "defoliated," exposed to ridicule, along with the myriad charred rabbit-shaped stumps at its foot. And so it would remain for an indeterminate period of time. On this continent this view of nakedness and ashes would reign for generations of onlookers. The few durmast oak shoots sprouting up from the debris would be buried again with each new rain shower. Even now, a few months after the great cat-

astrophe, heaps of marl lay at the base of the mountain to be carried off by the water and shifted to the
plains or to be sundered from the mountain by
avalanches of scree. The streams had left their beds
and trickled silently somewhere underground. This
stillness, as well as the trusted, mild breeze of the
highlands, no longer had any effect ("no longer
had any effect"?—was no longer present): no birds.
The entire region would no longer belong, however often he returned, to that which had helped
him search for the way: the land of cicadas. A gen-
eral deadness with no particular corpse of animal,
bird, or even cicada. Only the path itself was left,
even if shifted by the debris. However, it led
nowhere. Furthermore, because even the last bram-
blebush was burnt to the roots, one could now
walk anywhere, in any direction, through the vast
tract of land where the undergrowth had once
marked the way.

Despite his urge to turn around on the spot and
return to Aix, he continued on through the burnt
landscape, against his will and as if hypnotized by

nature-destroyed root and branch, now on truly pathless and porous earth that gave with each step. Under his feet the remains of roots appeared regularly, like sunken pilings. The storm that had followed the fire had washed many boulders from the earth. The rocks' surface was clearly dappled with dark gray and off-white. The scorching heat had chipped off the tops of the rocks in points and left behind this rhythmic pattern, (while) the bits of stone lay strewn about just as dappled but in a reverse pattern—light gray ashes and the light red marl. In the after image, this gigantic battery of shrapnel shot and swirled through the air as completely different balls of fire. Then the surrounding silence—no, not surrounding, there was no longer any specific area to be surrounded—was broken by a crashing and a crackling that grew into a great racket and ended with an explosion. Without any wind, a single, apparently still green tree fell and, torn in two, showed that the flames had devoured its core, there where the resin was probably most concentrated, and had left it a hollow black tube.

Here and there a timid attempt had been made at clearing up: a few stumps had been sawn off, a few enormous piles had been made. The last drops of resin oozed from deep within the remains of pine trees in thick white bubbles covering the dead wood in a soft, shimmering layer as thick as one's arm, occasionally bursting and beginning to flow sluggishly. Thick white streaks, like solid streaks of bad luck, appeared here and there on the bark-covered cylinders much wider and more regular than ever found on living trunks. Banners of soot blackened the wall of the fill dam built by Emile Zola's father, over the fjord-like gully: the storming fire had been so violent that it had even leapt over this considerable width of emptiness devoid of vegetation, spewing soot and staining the wall.

It then became clear, as he wandered through this destruction, stumbling, and at times even staggering dizzily, that with the burning of Mont Sainte-Victoire he had lost a path, a way, until then the only thing he had had of any permanence. It had been the only thing he could dependably recover. With each return, it had yielded in a new way some knowledge that, though it had always been present, had previously remained hidden. At the same time it also became clear to him that he had also lost all similar paths of the last few years: the path in the Yugoslavian karst because he was no longer a nameless wanderer and visitor of parks but the one who . . . , the way through the fields surrounding his hometown because all the paths there had been dug up or plowed under. . . . How strange then that this recognition of his paths' disappearance was not only accompanied by disappointment (in himself as well), anger (also with himself), and fear (of having no escape, of being unable to go on), but with an additional acquiescence.

Acquiescence? Resignation? But if resignation, why, then, "additional"? And another addition: always walking his paths alone, he had imagined a future in which he walked with another. Future? He ends with questions.